River City Editors

List, Sell, Profit

How to Really Make Money Selling on eBay

Table of Contents

Introduction

This book offers a straightforward no BS approach to selling on eBay.

What this book isn't.

This book isn't going to tell you how to become an eBay millionaire overnight, or promise you that you can become a top-rated eBay seller in ninety days. If that's what you're looking for, you can stop reading right now and request a refund from Amazon.

What this book is.

If on the other hand, you are willing to put in the time and effort necessary to build a business that will give you the extra money you need to go on a vacation every year, or drive a shiny new car every other year, this book can help you to reach these goals.

Making a side income of a few hundred or even a few thousand dollars a month is entirely doable. There are tens of thousands of people that do it every day, and you can too.

My goal in this book is to help you over some of the speed bumps that have stumped other sellers as they got started selling on eBay.

Who am I, and why should you listen to me

Hey there, Max Power here.

I've been selling on eBay for over fifteen years now. I'm a top rated eBay seller, and have completed nearly thirty thousand transactions on eBay in that time.

As you can guess, I've had my share of ups and downs, had my butt kicked more than once, but I never let any of that stop me. I've sold movies, books, and clothes, anything I thought might make me a profit.

You name it – I've given it a whirl on eBay.

I truly believe you can sell anything on eBay if you market it right. That means writing a great description that makes people drool and demand to know more about what you're selling. It means taking first rate photos that show your product from every angle; and finally, it means pricing your items to sell.

It sounds pretty easy, doesn't it?

Unfortunately, saying and doing, are two entirely different things. Most times you know exactly what you want to say, and the type of pictures you should use, they just get all scrambled up when you go to post them.

So in a way, what I'm going to teach you is something you already know.

Selling on eBay really is all about using good old common sense. You need to tell people what they want to know about the items you're selling, but you need to serve it up to them in a way that makes the whole package appear more attractive.

Think about when you shop at Walmart around Super Sunday, or any other major holiday. Pop, beer, and chips are all great sellers, but to really move them they need to add a little oomph. That's why the pop and beer displays are stacked to the ceiling, in the shapes of a football player, or the packaging is made to spell out the team name or city. That extra touch catches your eye, and makes you toss an extra case or two in your cart. And, oh yeah, better grab some of those chips they've got right next to it. That's the way you need to work eBay.

Your pictures and words are the building blocks for your display. The more professional your listings look and feel; the better the chance you will have to sell your item at a premium price.

Why eBay?

eBay is the giant on the block. They have 128 million active users that spent over $83 billion dollars in 2013, and they will gladly let you tap into that market for a small piece of the action.

The best part is, casual sellers can jump in and test the waters with no money up front. Each and every month sellers without an eBay store can list their first fifty items with no insertion fees.

Where else can you put your wares in front of 128 million active buyers without spending a single penny up front? There's a lot of talk out there about how you need to build your own website to strike it rich. The online "gurus" talk about building niche websites where you can put your product in front of internet shoppers. But have you ever given it a shot? It's like trying to draw your twelve year old away from the latest version of Call of Duty on their iPad. It's not going to happen.

What does a fisherman do when he wants to catch fish? He dangles his line where the fish are biting for other fishermen.

The same thing goes when you're selling online.

You can fight your way up stream against the current, or you can jump right in and drop your lure where the other sellers are already hooking buyers. The choice is yours, but if you want to reel in more sales – You've got to go where the buyers are. And, for the time being, eBay is one of the best spots on the internet to attract ready buyers eager to part with their cash.

My thought, and what has worked best for me, is to start on eBay. Build a business that you can be proud of, and when you're ready to spread your wings, test the waters on Amazon.

Look at it this way, in a recent survey conducted by Cowen Internet Retail Tracker in August of 2013, 53% of respondents made a purchase on Amazon, and 24% made a purchase on eBay. Only 11% made a purchase on Walmart.com and less than 7% purchased on Target.com.

If companies the size of Walmart and Target can only reach 11% of internet shoppers, what do you think your chances are of reaching anyone?

Let me say it again—start with eBay, spread out to Amazon when the time is right, and enjoy the sales they will bring to you.

Let's get started.

Where do you find stuff to sell?

Just about the first question every new eBay seller has is, "Where do I find stuff to sell?"

My answer to that question is to take a look around you. When I first started selling on eBay I sold things I already had around the house, books, sports cards, clothes, shoes, and a broken laptop. You name it, and you can probably sell it on eBay.

It really is crazy what people will spend their money on. You know the old saying, "One man's junk is another man's treasure." eBay proves that saying true every day.

If you haven't taken a good look at what's being offered on the site, you need to stop everything and spend a few hours cruising through listings. It's ok to start out looking at things you're interested in, but don't stop there.

You really need to browse the categories. Take a good look at some of the stuff people are listing. It will make you think twice the next time you haul your trash out to the curb.

Let me give you a few examples:

There's a guy in the book category who sells individual pages from a 1600's Bible for $25.00 to $75.00 per page depending upon the pictures on them. Dozens of people are selling old magazine articles or advertisements for from $10.00 to $50.00 each. Old Playboy magazines are selling starting at $5.00, and fashion magazines with pop stars on the cover start at $25.00.

Just about anything in the clothing category is going to find a ready buyer if you price it right. Smart sellers are pairing pieces together into outfits, or several pairs of slacks and blouses that can be mixed and matched for a week's worth of outfits. I know one guy who hits the local shoe stores every week for closeouts, and resells them on eBay for two to three times what he paid.

Another lady I know keeps an eye on the closeouts at Marshall's, T J Maxx, and the Gap. When the price is right she pounces on a whole cart full of fashions, and triples her money selling them on eBay.

Does your town have a Big Lots? How about a Target or Walmart?

Retail stores run a constant stream of clearance sales. There's nothing wrong with the items they're closing out. Sometimes the items don't sell fast enough to justify the shelf space. Other times they're seasonal items. At the end of the season the store needs to change inventory to maximize their sales potential, so the old items hit the clearance bin.

Next time you're at the store, grab your cell phone. Use the eBay or Amazon app and check what some of those clearance items are selling for online. It just may surprise you.

Sometimes regular price items can be just the ticket you need to rev up sales. One of my friends is a party planner. She helps mom's plan their kids birthday parties, and shops places like Party City for the best selection. About two years ago she got the idea to put together themed party packs and offer them for sale on eBay. Three thousand sales later her business is booming.

Here's what she does. She picks a theme, say Sponge Bob. Next she cruises the aisles searching for Sponge Bob related items: plates, napkins, party hats, party favor bags, wrapping paper, piñatas, and candy. She takes careful notes about what size packages they're offered in, prices, quantity discounts, etc.

After she picks out all the items, she heads home and prices out party packs for eight, twelve, and twenty-four kids. Her initial investment is minimal. She buys the smallest packages she can, shoots all of her pictures, and posts her listings framed in party templates. Most party packs let her double her investment; sometimes she can do a whole lot better when the stores are offering closeout specials.

Another friend of mine finds most of his inventory at pawn shops. He favors smaller items – jewelry, CD's, and DVD's. When he finds something he likes he talks to the manager about making a package deal. What kind of price can you give me if I buy twenty-five CD's? How about if I buy all of your DVD's? What the best price you can give me? Other times he can get the manager to bundle two or three pieces of jewelry into a package deal. You'd be surprised how many pawn shops are willing to deal with you when you can show them a stack of hundred dollar bills.

What's your passion?

Do you collect baseball cards? Stamps? Isabel Bloom statues? Chances are you're going to find a ready market on eBay if you can offer them at an attractive price.

Let's Start Selling

For the purposes of this book, I'm going to assume you already have an eBay and PayPal account. If you don't, you can follow these links to set up your accounts now.

Set up eBay account

https://scgi.ebay.com/ws/eBayISAPI.dll?RegisterEnterInfo

Set up PayPal account

https://www.paypal.com/uk/webapps/setup-paypal-account/onboarding?execution=e1s1

Both companies provide great directions, and it shouldn't take you over fifteen minutes to sign up for both services.

Getting Started

Selling on eBay can be broken down into six simple steps:

1) Create a killer title loaded with keywords that people can use to find your item.

2) Take accurate pictures that display your item in its best light.

3) Write a description that grabs the buyer's attention. It needs to answer any questions buyers may have about your item.

4) Price your item to sell.

5) Ship your items promptly and safely.

6) Customer service is everything. To continue growing your sales you need to maintain five-star feedback.

That's really all there is to it. Follow these six steps and you're going to make a lot of sales on eBay. Skimp on any of them, and your sales are going to suffer.

Let's investigate each of these areas and see what it takes to develop the best eBay listings possible.

Title

Your title contains the search terms that help buyers discover what you are selling.

A lot of seller's waste time trying to craft a great sounding title that reads like a perfect sentence. That's a big mistake. Your title has only one purpose – to help people find your item in eBay's search.

It needs to be loaded with relevant keywords that buyers can use to find your item. eBay only gives you eighty-eight characters to work with, so you need to make each one of them count.

Here are some of the terms you want to include in your title –

- Brand

- Model number

- Color

- Size

- Condition – New, used, or refurbished

- Short Description

- Men's, women's, children's

The key is to fit in as many keywords as you can into your title. Never abbreviate, unless it is a common abbreviation that everyone will understand. Some abbreviations that are unique to eBay are NWT (new with tags), NWB (new in box), BIN (Buy it Now), MNT (Mint), MIP (Mint in package), and OEM (Original equipment manufacturer). To see a more complete list, visit the link below.

http://pages.ebay.com/help/account/acronyms.html

Make sure you spell everything correctly, especially the product name, maker, and model number. People can't find your item if your keywords are misspelled.

Condition can be tricky. If your item is new, or used, say so. If it is refurbished, the method of refurbishment can be important. Suppose you're selling a refurbished iPad. You can say refurbished, factory refurbished, or Apple refurbished. Factory refurbished or Apple refurbished will be more important to most buyers.

Sometimes people need a little more information to decide what they want. If you're selling a Nook or a Kindle, you may also want to use the keywords e-reader and tablet to cover all of your bases. You may think of it as a Kindle, but a lot of people are looking for a basic e-reader or tablet and they won't be able to find your item if you don't include these keywords.

If you're selling clothes or shoes, people want to know the size, color, brand, model number, and whether it's for men, women, or children. Many sellers leave some of this information out because they think they have it covered in the description, the item specifics, or the category. Remember buyers will never get that far if they can't find your item in the first place. So pack everything you can into the title.

With all of that said, what's the best way to decide which keywords to include in your title?

Advanced research is the key to a great listing.

If you haven't used the advanced search feature before, you can find it at the top of the eBay screen. The word advanced is at the far right side of the search bar.

Click on it, and it will take you to the advanced search feature.

This will allow you to a do number of different searches. My advice is to type in three or four of your search terms, and then scroll down a few lines to where it says search including, and check the sold listings box. If you want to narrow your search even further you can choose the type of listing, auction or fixed price. You can also select the condition, new or used.

The searches eBay returns are only items that were recently sold. The benefit for you is you can see what worked for other sellers. Eliminate the items that sold for the most and the least. Concentrate on the middle listings first. What keywords did they use? Which keywords are common to all of the listings that sold? Now take a look a top three or four listings. Did they use any different keywords? Were they in a different sequence than the other listings used them in?

Write down the keywords that stick out. Also make a note of the item numbers for some of the better listings you see. We will be coming back to them later.

What we did here is really simple. Rather than guess at the keywords that sell, we found a list of the ones that actually made money for buyers. That gives us one of the building blocks we need to construct a great listing.

Pictures

Pictures can make or break your eBay listing.

On eBay you have two types of pictures: Galley pictures, and listing pictures.

The galley picture is the most important picture. It's what buyers see when they are cruising through the listings. You want it to be clear and focused. Get a good overall shot of the product you are selling. Do not include a close up of the product tag in your galley listing. eBay does not allow writing over photos, and sometimes they mistake an item tag for writing over the picture.

Pictures need to be at least 500 pixels on the longest side. eBay suggests 1600 pixels for the best quality. This way when people use the zoom feature they can view all of the details. Best advice, if you are using a digital camera to take your pictures use the medium or high resolutions settings. This will ensure that your pictures are always sized right. If you are scanning pictures, or using a smaller picture you can resize them with Paint or another graphics program.

When you're taking pictures think about what your buyers are going to need to see to make an informed decision. This means taking pictures from as many different angles as possible. If you have accessories such as a case, cord, ear buds, or packaging, get a separate shot of them.

If the item you're selling has damage, don't just describe it, show one or two pictures of the damaged area.

Let buyers decide for themselves whether the damage is a deal breaker, or not.

If you're selling clothes or anything with a fancy pattern be sure to show close up photos of the design work.

If you are selling coins, jewelry, or other small items consider using a light box. It will help you take close up photos so your customers can get a better view of what you're selling. You can find light boxes on eBay or Amazon starting at $29.99. Most of them come with several different colored backdrops and a tripod to help hold your camera steady.

One other key takeaway about photos—be sure to upload them through eBay's photo service. The advantage to doing this is they are optimized for mobile viewing. If you use a service like Auctiva, Vendio, or Inkfrog; they embed your pictures in the eBay listing. Many times these show up real small when viewed on a mobile device; other times they don't show up at all.

The reason this is so important is last year 27 percent of online sales occurred on mobile devices, this year that number is expected to be 40 percent or more. If you don't use eBay's picture service you could be eliminating nearly half of your potential buyers.

Description

Your description is the meat and potatoes of your listing. A great description encourages buyers to click on the buy button; a so-so description encourages them to move on to the next listing.

So how do you write a great description?

You need to think about your buyer. Why would they want your item? What are they going to do with it?

What kind of problems is it going to solve for them?

Sure, it may only be an iPad. But for your potential buyer it's a solution to his mobile computing needs. He can use it on the go. Pull up needed information during sales meetings. Play games or check email while he's riding the subway.

To write a great description you need to keep this information in the back of your head.

You also need to focus on the item.

If you're selling a World War II era bomber jacket, you need to talk about the condition of the jacket. What condition is the leather in? Is it peeling or chipping? How about the artwork? Is it free of blemishes? Does it feature a pinup girl, a bomber, or a group insignia?

Be sure to describe the item completely. Make sure that you tell the good, the bad, and the ugly. If there's a big rip in the lining, tell buyers (show them a picture too).

Buyers don't like surprises. They expect that old items will have a few problems. This isn't usually an issue, unless you don't tell them about it.

Sellers worry that telling people their item has a few flaws will kill the sale. Buyers worry that sellers aren't being entirely truthful with them. The easiest way to make your description more believable is to tell people your item has a few problems.

It's all in how you approach it.

You don't want to come out and say your item is crap. You want to describe what's good about it first. Build your item up. Make it shine, and then say, oh, by the way…

Here's how you can do that.

iPad 2. I've had this baby for two years now and it's really done a great job for me. It comes with the original box, charger, and ear buds. It has 32 Gigs of memory, so there's plenty of room to store all of your music and videos. I will throw in the Otterbox case to help you keep it safe. It does have a small scratch in the lower right hand part of the screen, I think that can be polished out, but I've never had the chance to try. Check out picture number three, and you can see what you think. Any questions? Just email me. I'll be happy to get you an answer.

It's short. Talks about the good stuff first, and mentions the scratch, and references a picture you can see it in. Then the seller invites questions.

Here's another description that downplays the damage.

I've got this old book from the Spanish American War. It's pretty fragile, the date on it is 1898. As you can see from the pictures, the pages are separating at the spine. The leather rubs, and you're going to get some brown flakes on your stuff when you're looking at it. The text and pictures are awesome. It's an oversize book, 11 x 16, so you really get some close up shots with the pictures. My favorite ones are the color drawings of the marines and cavalry on the battlefields. I've included a few color pictures of the battleships, too. One even shows them firing a torpedo. I almost hate to part with this one, but the wife says we need a few bucks more for that Caribbean cruise we're taking. You know the old saying, one man's loss, is another man's gain.

Don't let this one pass you by.

It's a great description. It's casual, talks about the book, and its flaws. More importantly it's enthusiastic.

"What I really like are these pictures." "One of them shows…" And, it ends with a call to action, "Don't let this one pass you by."

Compare that with the normal drab descriptions most sellers use, and you can understand why this book sold for a premium price.

With that said, how do you write the best description possible?

My thought is, it should be short. One or two paragraphs is best. If you have a lot of information, or item details you need to include, use a series of short bullet points.

This is the internet age. Most people don't read.

They scan your listing to quickly find the information they're looking for. You can help them find it by not writing long detailed descriptions. Instead, use a series of headings, followed by bullet points for each section. This is the way people read web pages and blog posts, and it's the way most people read eBay listing descriptions.

You should also skip all of the disclaimers, about shipping, payment information, auction terms, etc. This stuff just takes up space. Instead enter all of your payment and shipping info in the item details. List your return policy in the proper section. This ensures your listing description contains only the information a buyer needs to make a decision.

Price

Price can make or break the deal.

If you price your item too high, your item is not going to sell; if you price it too low, you're going to leave money on the table.

So what do you do?

Sellers have their own pricing theories. Some sellers set an arbitrary price. I want to get $25.00 for that.

Other seller's set their prices based upon their costs. If they pay $20.00 for an item, they want to double or triple their money, and price accordingly. A few sellers like to pick crazy prices, and put them out there hoping to make a few big scores. You see this on Amazon and eBay a lot in the book categories. Most sellers offer a book for five or ten bucks, and down at the bottom of the list there are several sellers offering the same book for $100.00, or even $500.00. Does it work? Sometimes. Will it work for you? Maybe.

My suggestion is to try different pricing models, and discover what works best for you.

Professional sellers price their items differently.

They research everything to make sure they get the best price possible for their items.

Let's go back to our advanced research example earlier in this book. When you search for items by closed sales, you know exactly what items similar to yours have recently sold for.

What does that tell you?

You know the exact price items in similar condition recently sold for. There's no guessing. You know what real people are willing to pay for your item.

You can drill down further, and look at just auctions. This gives you a chance to determine what the best starting price is for your item. Let's look at iPhone's.

The iPhones that sold for the highest price, started at 99¢, or $9.99. The iPhones that started at these prices sold for the most money, and received the most bids.

We can also see that iPhones that started at $99.99, $299.00, or more; all received fewer bids, and sold for less than iPhones that started at a lower price. That tells us if we want to get the best possible price, we need to start our iPhone at 99¢, and let the market set the price.

Is there an element of risk involved in starting your item at 99¢? Yes, but it's not as great as you may think.

Your research gives you a good idea of the price range your item should sell in. iPhones and other electronics usually sell in a tight price range, so you can expect to get a few bucks on either side of the median price. Sometimes the range is wider than you expect. It just depends on how many items are closing when yours is, and how many bidders are active at the time.

If you sell most of your items at fixed price, advanced research can still be a big help.

Search by sold items that sold at fixed price. This will return a list of items that sold, how much they sold for, and if they were listed with a buy it now. If they sold using a buy it now, you can see what price the item actually sold for.

Another way to set your fixed price is to look at what similar items sold for at auction, and set your buy it now price just under the top prices the item sold for at auction. Then add a best offer, and set it to accept at the lowest price you're willing to take.

Sometimes advanced research can't help you.

If you sell unique items that have never sold before, or sell infrequently, you may have to wing it.

Look at what similar items have sold for, or take a stab at it, and guess. What's the worst that can happen? Your item doesn't sell, and you reprice it. Or, you sell your item for less than the prime dollar, but you still make money.

If you have a number of similar items to sell, list them at different prices. Then run with the price that brings you the most sales.

Unique items pose an additional challenge for sellers who like to price everything starting at 99¢ and let the market set the price. If the buyers don't materialize for your item, it's going to sell for 99¢ or $1.04.

Here's a warning for sellers.

If you have a one of a kind item, starting your auction at 99¢ can be the worst decision you ever make. A better strategy would be to start your item at the lowest price you are willing to accept for it. This protects you from the unexpected.

Shipping

S hipping can be one of the easiest parts of selling on eBay, or it can be a major time suck. It's all in how you handle it.

The good thing is eBay has developed a number of tools to make shipping easy. Sellers can ship items directly from the eBay listing, or from the PayPal payment page.

Both methods make shipping a breeze.

Before we go into any more details about shipping methods, I want to take a few moments to explain shipping policies that will affect you on eBay.

As a seller, you are responsible for the items you sell arriving safely and on time. eBay and PayPal require certain shipping standards for items, based upon the value of the item you sell.

Sellers can no longer charge buyers for insurance on shipments. You need to roll insurance costs into your shipping price.

While tracking isn't required on most shipments, it protects you, and the buyer from common shipping snafus.

The least you need to know is you should describe all damage to items correctly and accurately in your listing descriptions. This will eliminate many common misunderstandings buyers have when they receive your item.

Before you list any item on eBay you want to take a few moments to think about shipping. Ask yourself if it will ship in an envelope, a padded mailer, a box, or a larger crate. Is it fragile? If so, then you will probably need bubble wrap, packing peanuts, or some kind of padding material. If it's a photo or magazine, you're going to need a stay flat mailer, or some other type of sturdy cardstock wrapper. Larger items may require special crating and pickup by a common carrier.

Understanding how you're going to ship your item and all of the required shipping materials will help you determine the proper fees to charge for shipping.

I recommend purchasing a shipping scale to weigh your items before you list them. Add an extra ½ pound or pound for packing materials, tape, and labels. This will give you the information you need to complete your listing.

Flat rate or calculated eBay offers two types of shipping – flat rate, and calculated.

Flat rate shipping is where you set one price to ship an item, and it is the same for everyone who purchases your item. If you're selling smaller low value items like postcards or single baseball cards, you may ship them in a small stay flat envelope. If you're selling rare Hummel figurines or other collectible that require padding and sturdy boxes, flat rate shipping may still be a good option because it will allow you to roll in the cost of packing materials and insurance.

Calculated shipping works with eBay's shipping calculator. It determines shipping prices for customers, based upon their zip codes and the weight of the items you are shipping. This is good for sellers of clothes, shoes, etc., or any other heavy and bulky items. Buyers who live closer to you will receive a better shipping rate than someone who lives further away. This will give you a competitive advantage with buyers living closer to you.

Combined Shipping Discount

Another option you need to consider is if you would like to offer a Combined Shipping Discount. What this does is let you offer discounted shipping to buyers when they purchase two or more items. Let's say you're selling books. If you charge $4.00 to ship the first book, you can offer to combine shipments and send all additional purchases for no additional shipping charge. Or you can discount shipping on additional items by $1.00 or $2.00. This encourages customers to purchase more items so they can save on shipping.

The easiest way to add a combined shipping discount is when you are listing your items on eBay. First, list your regular shipping price. After you do this, the box next to it is for shipping for additional purchases. If you type in zero, the cost to ship additional items is free. If you type in $1.00, $2.00, or another number, this is what your customer will be charged to ship additional items.

When you offer a combined shipping discount eBay invoices your buyer with the correct shipping amount (less all discounts). You don't need to make any adjustments before your buyers can make a payment. The other option is to manually send corrected invoices to your buyers. Just know this will cause confusion, and leave you with some angry customers. Some of them will pay the full shipping charge, and expect you to refund the difference. Others will delay payments waiting for you to correct the invoice for them. To prevent these problems, set your shipping options up properly when you first list your items.

Tracking and Signature Tracking

Best practices are to include tracking with every item you send.

It saves you having to answer buyer inquiries about when they will receive their item. And, it keeps everyone involved in the transaction honest. Sometimes customers say they didn't get the item you sent. Sometimes another family member picks up the item and forgets to tell your customer it arrived.

Tracking shows two things: 1) that your item was mailed, and 2) that it was delivered to the customer's house. The way this works is the Post Office scans the item when you drop it off. Many times they scan the package along the way, so you can see the various points it travels through. The mailman makes a final scan when he leaves your package at the customer's home. This is called proof of delivery.

A lot of times when a customer says they did not receive an item, tracking will give you clues to where the item is. Many times, you will see that the mailman attempted to deliver your package but no one was home to receive it. Instead the mailman left a tag telling the customer they need to pick the package up at the post office. When this happens, you can tell the customer they need to contact their local post office to arrange pickup.

Other times, the post office says the address you shipped your package to is an invalid or incorrect address.

Tracking will show that it is being returned to you. Again, you can explain to your customer what is happening.

If your customer doesn't receive their package, the first thing eBay is going to do is ask you to upload the tracking number. If you do, and the tracking info shows delivered, you win. They cancel the case against you. If you can't provide tracking info or proof of delivery, the customer wins, and you will be forced to refund the purchase price plus shipping.

Sometimes you have tracking and the item still goes astray. The post office scans it in when you drop it off for delivery, and it disappears from sight after that. You can ask your local post office to check the dead letter office, but most often your package is gone. You will need to refund your buyer or send a new item.

When you're shipping an item valued at over $200.00 eBay and PayPal require signature delivery. Signature delivery requires the customer, or someone at that address to personally sign for the package when it is delivered. If you just use regular postal tracking you could be forced to refund your customer if they say they didn't receive the item, even if it shows delivered.

Be sure to ship everything using the proper services.

Customer Service

To really be successful on eBay you need to show buyers you can play well with other members of the eBay community.

How do you do that?

Write complete descriptions that accurately describe what you're selling – warts and all. Provide large close-up pictures of what you are selling. Respond quickly to customer inquiries. Cheerfully accept returns, even when you know the damage or other problems aren't your fault.

Apologize. Apologize. Apologize often.

Say I'm sorry. Say it again.

Take the blame even when you know that it's not your fault.

Think of yourself like a busy waitress on a Saturday evening. People are stacked up twenty deep waiting for a table. It is 10° below zero, and the line outside is getting longer. Two waitresses called in sick, you've got a new bartender who doesn't know the difference between a strawberry daiquiri and mint julep, and there are three babies in line, and you're out of high chairs. Who's going to explain it to those parents?

Are you starting to get the idea?

Selling on eBay is hectic! You're trying to take pictures, post new auctions, and set up a weekend sale.

You just received three emails from customers who received the wrong item. They're screaming mad, and they want the right item today. And, to top it off, UPS just delivered a shipment of broken widgets you were supposed to have in the mail yesterday.

Think it can't happen?

Several times a year I hear from customers I messed up and shipped them the wrong item. All of a sudden it's a mad scramble to get everything back, apologize profusely, and track everything down so I can straighten out this hot pile of doo doo.

So what do you do?

After you've been at it awhile, and been through the same crisis several times things get easier to handle. Customer service comes first. In the above example, I would suggest stopping everything. Apologize to the customer who said he received the wrong item. It can be something as simple as, "Sorry for the mix-up. Sometimes things go astray, and I'll do everything I can to take care of this for you. If you can get that item on the way back to me, I'll track down your item, and get it to you as quick as I can. Or, if you prefer, I will be glad to offer you a full refund. Just mail back the item you received. Thanks again for your understanding. It was entirely my fault."

That's the easy part. Now you want to jump ahead and do some damage control. Find out what item the customer received. Send a quick email to the person who should have received it. Let them know you experienced a shipping snafu, and they will be receiving the wrong item.

Again, let them know you are sorry for the mix-up, and that you will gladly cover shipping both ways, offer a full refund, or both. Most customers understand that mistakes happen.

It's easier to accept when you apologize and put all of the blame on yourself. It diffuses the customer's anger.

Why is this so important?

eBay operates on a five-star feed-back system. The better your feed-back score, the higher your items will rank in search. Because of this, you need to do everything you can to protect your feed-back rating.

Five star feed-back is your goal. Realistically, that's an impossible number to maintain, especially when you're selling hundreds or thousands of items per month.

In an ideal world four star feed-back would be amazing. In eBay's convoluted grading system it gets a little weird. Sellers are expected to maintain a 4.8 rating or better. Anything less than 4.6 can get your selling privileges suspended or revoked. Because of this it's important to do everything you can to protect your feed-back.

When you get a complaint, suck it in. Apologize; take the blame; offer a refund. Do whatever it takes to keep your customer happy. Any hit you take to maintain customer satisfaction will pay off with a higher feed-back rating and more sales down the road.

A lot of sellers mention in their eBay listings that they strive for five star feed-back. "We strive for five star feed-back. If for any reason you feel you cannot leave five star feed-back for us, please contact us and we will do whatever we can to make it right." Other sellers send a postcard or business card that mentions how important it is to their continued success on eBay that buyers leave five star feed-back for them.

In my book, that's crossing the line. But, you have to do what you have to do to retain a high feedback rating.

The best assurance that you will rank highly, is to treat customers like you would expect to be treated.

Why you need an eBay store

If you really want to make money selling on eBay, you need to open an eBay store.

An eBay store is your own little place on the internet. It shows customers you are serious about selling.

More importantly, it gives you a chance to brand yourself, and showcase the items you sell.

Let's start with the basics. eBay sellers can choose from three levels of stores.

Basic store

- $19.99 per month
- Includes up to 200 free listings
- Excellent for new sellers, or sellers with a limited product line

Premium store

- $59.99 per month
- Includes up to 500 free listings
- Great for intermediate sellers

Anchor Store

- $199.99 per month
- Includes up to 2500 free listings
- Excellent for sellers with a large inventory of items, or for sellers interested in moving a large quantity of product.

Store branding

When you operate an eBay store, it lets you brand your business. It gives you a place to keep all of your items together, and make it easier for customers to find them.

How do you do this?

An eBay store lets you build a custom showcase for your items. You can use graphics and words to describe your business, and give customers a more enticing look at what you are selling.

Some of the better eBay storefronts have custom graphics for every category of item they are selling, along with a short description of the products included in that category. They have a tagline in their header that describes their business, business philosophy, or a short quote that describes their business.

An eBay store lets you break your business down into categories. Customers can use these categories to more easily find items that fit their interests. In my case, I have the categories displayed to the left of my listings and store page so that customers can readily access them.

Include a search bar in your store header. This makes it easy for customers to find items in your eBay store. More importantly, it keeps customers from searching all of eBay, and losing track of your items.

Mark down manager

When you have an eBay store you have access to a feature called Mark down manager. Mark down manager lets sellers discount items in their eBay store for a select period of time. If you haven't tried it yet, it's a great way to increase sales and move slow selling product.

The way mark down manager works is sellers select a start and end date for their sale. After that you select a discount amount. You can set the discount as a percentage, a specific dollar amount, or you can offer free shipping. Next you choose which listings you would like to discount. You can offer all listings from a specific category, all fixed price listings, all auction style listings, or you can select individual listings. A few exceptions apply. If you use mark down manager to discount auction listings, the only option you have is to offer free shipping. The number of listings you can discount at any one time is determined by the store subscription you have.

Finally, you are given an option to promote your sale. If you've collected an email list of customers who would like to stay in contact with you on eBay, you can send a short newsletter announcing your sale. This will get the ball rolling and help to bring in interested customers.

My suggestion is to offer a discount every week. It can be on just a few items, or you can rotate through categories. It doesn't have to be a big discount; sometimes

I've drawn a great response offering as little as seven to eleven percent off of my regular prices.

Give mark down manager a whirl and see what it can do for your business.

Take advantage of promotional boxes

Promotional boxes let you call out special features of your business. You can ask customers to sign up for your email list; mention combined shipping discounts; talk about new items you added to your store this week; post a quote of the week that may get people to keep coming back and see what's next.

I use promotional boxes to let customers know I'm running a sale. I have a sidebar featured below my category list that tells customers a little more about my business, and why they may be interested in the items I'm selling.

Take a few moments now and then to explore what other sellers are doing, and incorporate some of those ideas into your promotion boxes.

Store reports

eBay offers a wealth of sales and traffic reports to help you grow your store sales.

Sales reports give you a quick three month overview of your business. You can see at a glance how many sales you made each month, how much you paid in fees, and unpaid item reports opened and closed during the period.

Traffic reports give you a good look at how many buyers are visiting your eBay listings, which pages they visit most often, and how many people are taking time out to view your store home page.

It gives you a good idea of what people are looking at now, and how much traffic your eBay listings are actually generating.

Put it all together and an eBay store gives you a great opportunity to power up your business.

If you want to make money selling on eBay, you need an eBay store. There's no way around it.

Try selling on Amazon

After you have your eBay store setup and running smoothly it's time to think about what's next.

Amazon is the logical next choice for most eBay sellers. There are a number of great tools that will transfer all of the items in your eBay store to Amazon, with little or no effort.

I've had the best luck with Bonanza. They synchronize your listings across platforms, and you are only charged when your items sell.

Check the information out here.
https://www.bonanza.com/booths/amazon_item_import/bonzuser_bmjwj

For most sellers, listing your items on Amazon using Bonanza is a two-step process. First, you import all of your eBay items into Bonanza. To get started you need to verify your eBay store info. After this you're given the opportunity to discount your items on Bonanza. Then you are offered an option to import your eBay feedback. I would recommend this.

After you click import, it can take several hours to a day to import all of your items from eBay. It depends upon how many items you have in your store. Be careful to only select import eBay items once. I got impatient, and clicked the button five times. That imported all of my items five times, so I ended up having to delete 30,000 items and start over again.

When all of your items are imported from eBay you're ready to transfer your items to Amazon. The first step is to connect your Amazon account with your Bonanza account. After you've done that, check off the following boxes where it says import options.

> Keep my Bonanza listings synchronized to my Amazon store.

> Revise items

This will transfer your items on Bonanza into your Amazon store, and keep them synched between eBay, Amazon, and Bonanza as you make sales and post new items for sale.

. . . .

Export Your Store is another company that will transfer all of your items from eBay to Amazon. Their service is more expensive. It starts at $299, and runs $99 per month to synch your items between sites.

. . . .

You're going to experience a few glitches when you use either service.

Amazon is a completely different animal than eBay. They are a marketplace. As such, all sellers sell from the same listing page. Because of this personal branding is not allowed.

If you sell one-of-a-kind items, Amazon handles them differently than eBay.

On Amazon if you have a unique item you need to set up a custom listing page. Both services do this when they transfer your items to Amazon.

When Bonanza, or Export Your Store, transfers your items to Amazon they need to strip out all of the HTML code used in your listings. Sometimes this goes smoothly; sometimes the ride can be a little bumpy. What happened to me with both services is a number of my listings were transferred over with just the title, price, and pictures.

None of the item descriptions came through. As a result I had to go back through every listing and edit hundreds of them.

Best advice: If you are synching a large number of items between sites, allow yourself plenty of time to check them out and make any corrections needed.

25 Tips & tricks to boost your sales

Here are some tips that can help you sell more, work faster, and make more money. Some are simple ideas you can use from day one, others will make more sense as you scale and grow your eBay business.

1) Set up a basic accounting system from day one. Your eBay life will run a lot smoother if you have a bookkeeping system in place from day one. It doesn't have to be anything sophisticated, just a simple way to record all of your sales and expenditures. That way when tax time comes around, you have all of the information you need close at hand.

My first bookkeeping system was a simple Excel spreadsheet. I used it to track my purchases, sales, and profits. I printed off all of my PayPal receipts and stored them in a three ring binder.

As time went by I transitioned to Quick Books, and then to Go Daddy Bookkeeping. Each of these solutions made the process simpler by automating my everyday accounting tasks.

Take some time now to set-up your accounting system.

2) Automate your feedback. Several apps will let you post feedback as soon as a buyer pays for your items. I use to

think it was important to leave all of my feedback personally, but when I started selling 700 to 800 items per month leaving feedback became a burden.

3) Use eBay's shipping tools. Shipping can easily become one of the biggest time sucks for eBay sellers. When you use eBay's shipping service it automatically transfers addresses and other information over to the labels it prints. Most shipping options also offer free or discounted tracking on your packages, plus they transfer the tracking info directly into the listing so buyers can check the progress of their shipments. This means fewer questions for you to answer about when customers are going to receive their shipment.

4) Use free packing materials from the USPS. If you ship by priority mail, get your boxes and envelopes free from the post office. They will even deliver them to you for free. Visit the following link for details https://store.usps.com/store/browse/category.jsp?categoryId=catGetMailingShippingSupplies&categoryNavIds=catgetMailingShippingSupplies

5) Stop going to the post office. If you're shipping by priority mail, the post office will pick up your packages. You can schedule delivery by following this link https://tools.usps.com/go/ScheduleAPickupAction!input.action

6) Take advantage of free listing days. eBay runs a number of free listing promotions every month. Take advantage of as many of them as you can to save on fees. I have a Premium eBay Store which means I receive 500 free listings each month. Additional listings are 10¢ each for fixed price or auction listings. Many months, eBay offers 500 to 2500 free listings. At 10¢ that's a savings of $50 to $250 per month.

Do the math before you list, or relist any items.

Sometimes you may need to let your items sit for a week or so while you wait for the next special to roll around.

(eBay has scaled way back on free listing promotions since I first wrote this. Occasionally you can still snag a free listing promotion for 500 or 1000 free auction listings, but they are few and far between compared to what they used to be.)

7) Offer free shipping. If it makes sense offer free shipping on your items. eBay loves free shipping and will promote your items more often when you offer free shipping.

8) Offer a combined shipping discount. If offering free shipping doesn't work for what you sell, consider offering a combined shipping discount to buyers who purchase more than one item. You'd be surprised at how many buyers will pick up another item or two when they can get free or discounted shipping on the additional items.

9) Respond quickly to buyer inquiries. Answer questions as quickly as you can. Potential buyers will lose interest if you make them wait to long for an answer. Unhappy customers will be delighted if you answer quickly, and let them know you're eager to help them solve their problem.

When you respond to customers be positive. Thank them for writing you and let them know it is a really great item. If a potential buyer wants to know something about your item, give them a little more information than they asked for.

Suppose a customer asks about the battery life on your iPad. Tell them, "It's a really nice iPad, with hardly any signs of wear. I mainly used it between classes. The only reason I'm getting rid of it is my parents gave me a new iPad

Air for my birthday. The battery lasts about ten hours if you're just listening to music or surfing the web."

The extra information may tip the scales and help them decide to buy your item.

If it's a buyer who's unhappy with a recent purchase, let them know you're there to help and that you understand their frustration. "Thank you for contacting me about your recent purchase. I'm very sorry to hear that you are unhappy with your item. I'll be glad to do whatever I can to make it right for you. Here are a few tips that may help…"

The main thing to remember is to say thank you often. Offer to help with any problems the buyer may have. If it's a potential customer and they're on the line about whether the item will work for their intended use, or about the condition, I make sure to mention my 100 percent money back guarantee. That takes all of the risk out of the deal.

10) Sell International. eBay has a new Global Shipping Program that makes shipping internationally as easy as shipping in the United States. The way it works is you opt into the program when you list your item. When the item sells, eBay collects shipping, fees, and customs duties from your customer. After this is done they provide you with the address of a shipping center within the United States to send your package to. As soon as your package is received at eBay's shipping center, your part in the transaction is complete.

From this point on eBay readdresses the package, and forwards it to your customer. They fill out all of the customs forms, choose the right shippers, and complete all of the heavy lifting for you.

If you haven't opted into the Global Shipping Program yet, give it a shot. Once I started selling internationally sales jumped thirty to thirty-five percent.

11) Setup your customer FAQ. Let eBay automatically answer common questions for you when buyers inquire about shipping, payment, combined shipping, item details, and returns. eBay answers these questions by responding with information you provided when listing your items. If you want to add additional info, you are allowed to do that as well.

Follow this link to activate your customer FAQ's.
http://contact.ebay.com/ws/eBayISAPI.dll?ManageSellerFAQ#Shipping

12) Accept returns. eBay doesn't require you to accept returns, but you should be aware that a liberal return policy will help you make more sales.

Face it buying online is scary, especially when you are purchasing used items sight unseen. When you offer a refund people feel better about buying from you. Often times just knowing they can return an item, will give buyers that extra nudge they need to purchase from you.

Many sellers are afraid to offer refunds because they feel it is one more way buyers can take advantage of them. I've offered a 100 percent money back guarantee for the past seven years, and have had fewer than 25 returns in all of that time.

All I'm saying is if you really want to make more sales, try offering a refund policy and see what it does for your sales.

13) Add video to your listings. It's a fact. People love video. If you can find a way to add videos to your listings, sales are going to go up.

It doesn't have to be a major production. Shoot a quick selfie video from your iPhone talking about your listing. If you've got something really cool like a model airplane or remote control car, show someone putting it through its paces.

You can even make it real simple and just introduce yourself, and what you like about selling on eBay. It will help build trust in you, which should lead to making more sales.

The best way to add video to your listing is to upload it to You Tube, and use the embed code to paste it into your listing page.

One quick note: Be sure to use the old embed code option. It works best with eBay.

14) Skip listing upgrades. You can do without most of eBay's listings upgrades. All they do is put extra money in eBay's pocket. The only one I would suggest is subtitle, and then only when you are selling an expensive item.

What subtitle does is give you an extra 88 characters to help describe your item. Words in your subtitle don't show up in search, but when buyers find your item, it gives them a little more information that may make them click into your items. Keep in mind if your item doesn't sell, it's going to cost an extra $1.50 when you relist your item, so be sure to remove the subtitle if you don't want to pay for it again.

15) Include tracking with all of your shipments.

Shipments get lost. Sometimes buyers say they didn't receive your item, when they did. Tracking keeps everybody honest. If buyers don't receive their package they can open an "item not received case against you."

The first thing eBay is going to do is ask for tracking information. If it shows delivered, you win the case. If you don't have tracking information, eBay will take the buyers word that they did not receive your package and refund the cost of your item plus shipping.

16) Set an insure limit. As a seller you are responsible for the buyer receiving the item in the condition you advertised it in. If the buyer doesn't receive the item, or it arrives broken, you are responsible. Set a limit that you're comfortable losing. Insure any packages that exceed that amount. Fifty dollars has always been my limit. If I ship packages valued at over fifty dollars I insure them. This way I limit my losses if something goes wrong.

You also need to keep in mind that eBay no longer allows sellers to charge for insurance. You need to roll the cost of insurance into your shipping price.

17) Sell in a variety of formats. Don't limit yourself to auctions or fixed price listings. Shake things up a bit. Be sure to use best offer, and buy it now.

If you have a large quantity of an item, try one day, three day, five day, seven day, and ten day auctions. Offer one item at auction, and sell a few more at fixed price. Tell people in your auction listing if they want the item now you also have it available with a buy it now.

You never know until you try.

Some buyers enjoy the thrill of bidding. They want to score a bargain. Other buyers just want to purchase the item they want and get it over with. Make sure you are catering to both types of buyers.

18) Try new things. Don't be afraid to experiment. Try new products. Keep the ones that sell, discard the ones that don't. Doing this will keep your inventory fresh, and assure you a constant stream of new products that keep customers coming back to see "what's next."

19) Keep an eye on your competition. If you really want to increase your sales, you need to keep an eye on your competition. Watch what they're selling. Keep an eye on any new product offerings they have. Know when they drop a product line. Keep an eye on their prices. Are they going up? Down? Or are they running a string of specials?

All of this is important information that can help you sell more stuff.

Several years ago my sales dropped significantly for about two months. Finally it got to the point I needed to figure out what was going on. After a bit of searching I discovered one of my competitors was getting ready to close his eBay store. He'd dropped his prices from $20.00 each to $2.00, and then $1.00. I couldn't match his prices. But, I did decide this was an opportunity for me to cherry pick his inventory. Over the next few weeks I grabbed five hundred items that made me a great profit once he was done selling out.

My suggestion is you should make a list of your top five competitors. At least once a month you should take a close look at what they are doing. Make some notes, and try some of the things they are doing. Over the long run, it will make you a better seller.

20) Set regular office hours. There's a danger to working at home. Because you have everything there, you are tempted to keep working at it longer than you should. You know what I mean. I just need to list five more sales. I just received a dozen new emails I better answer them quick.

And, then, there's the biggest time waster of all constantly checking sales. I admit I still have a problem with this one.

If you can do it, set a time limit. Tell yourself I'm shutting eBay off at 7:00 so I can spend time with my family. So I can read a good book. So I can go jogging.

One of the best things you can do is to find a good work / life balance.

21) Read a lot of books. To be successful you need to read. Read a lot of books about how to sell on eBay. Even the worst ones will give you two or three pieces of advice that can help you make more sales.

Read about what you sell. The more you know about the product line you sell the more you are going to sell. Buyers love buying from an expert. The more you know about your product line, the more pertinent information you will be able to put in your listings.

Being an expert is also going to help you make smarter purchases. If you shop at garage sales, estate sales, or auctions, you're going to recognize bargains. As a result, you should make more money.

22) Write eBay reviews and guides. Share your knowledge with others. eBay guides and reviews give you the opportunity to position yourself as an expert in what you sell.

Writing them doesn't have to be time consuming.

Do you sell DVD's? Did you watch a new movie? Write a short review telling people what you liked about it. Over time it's easy to post hundreds of reviews. As readers stumble across them many will check out your eBay store.

Some may even make a purchase or two.

Do you sell stamps, coins, or baseball cards?

Millions of collectors visit eBay everyday looking for these items. If you write a few guides about grading, collecting tips, how to get the best deal at auction, etc., potential buyers are going to look at you as an expert. Many of them will check out what you're selling.

Use eBay guides and reviews to grow your business.

23) Fill out your eBay profile. Profiles are new to eBay this year. Similar to the old MY World, Profiles lets you share information about yourself with other eBay buyers and sellers.

This feature is eBay's attempt to join the social networking revolution. At the top of your Profile page you have the opportunity to post your profile picture, and behind it a banner. You get a short spot to describe your business, and then it shows your feedback.

Below this eBay shows five items you are selling in a scroll bar that allows sellers to look through your items.

The next section is for collections, another new eBay feature. Collections are a Pinterest like feature that let you build picture collections of items you are selling, or other items you like that are selling on eBay.

Below that is a section for followers, and then a larger section that shows your eBay reviews and guides.

My advice is to fill out as much of your eBay Profile as you can. People like to know who they're dealing with. The more you can show them you are a real person, the more people will buy from you.

24) End your items often. Cassini Search has a preference for new items. If you have an eBay store with hundreds or thousands of fixed priced listings, end them often. Instead of using good-till-cancelled, list your items for thirty days.

This will ensure your items stay fresh.

The advantage to you is your items will rise in search each time you relist them. As a result you should make more sales.

25) Develop an inventory system. One of my biggest challenges occurred about six month after I started selling on eBay. I moved from listing one hundred items per month to listing over five thousand items.

It was nearly impossible to find items when the time came to ship them. Some days it took me longer to locate all of the items I sold than it did to print the labels.

I was selling videos, and they were in boxes scattered all across the basement. Finally, I decided that's enough! I went out and bought a dozen shelves. I labeled them from A to Z and got everything together. It made life a lot easier and saved me over an hour a day in shipping time.

When boxes of videos came in I scanned them, and put them on the proper shelves.

My advice is to develop a good inventory and storage system from day one. It will make your life easier over the long run.

Final Advice

Selling on eBay isn't for the faint of heart. Some months you make a lot of money, other months it's like getting a tooth pulled. It hurts. Bad!

The trick is to stay in the game for the long haul. Over time you can make more, and more money, selling on eBay, just by running a constant stream of listings.

When I first started selling on eBay, most weeks I would list five or ten items. Some weeks, I decided not to list any more items because it was too much work, or last week's listings hadn't sold well. So I figured, what the hell, why bother. Today, I know that kind of thinking is a mistake.

If you expect to be successful selling on eBay, you need to post a steady stream of listings. Just by posting listings every week, you're going to make more sales. More listings, means more eyes on the items you're selling. Even if you don't sell anything today, a certain number of buyers are going to like what they see, and bookmark your listings so they can see what's next.

And, that brings up my next two points.

1. If you don't currently have an eBay store, you need to start one now.

2. You need to pick out a product line, and stick with it.

I don't think I would have been as successful selling on online as I was if I hadn't opened an eBay store, and begun specializing in a single product line. As soon as I opened my eBay store, it let people know I was serious about what I was doing. It also gave me a place to pack away all of those listings that didn't sell from week to week.

A lot of sellers cut their losses after they run an item once or twice. I used to be the same way, but I learned from experience—it's not the item, you just have to wait for the right buyer to come along.

Every item has its time. Once the right buyer comes along, it's going to sell. Most often for full price.

If I had to sum it up, that's the whole secret to success on eBay. Keep your hand in the game by listing items regularly, and specialize in one product line early in your career. If you do these two things, you're going to succeed.